SPECTRUM®

Writing

Grade 2

Published by Spectrum®
an imprint of Carson Dellosa Education
Greensboro, NC

Spectrum® is an imprint of Carson Dellosa Education.

Printed in the United States of America. All rights reserved. Except as permitted under the United States Copyright Act, no part of this publication may be reproduced or distributed in any form or by any means, or stored in a database or retrieval system, without prior written permission from the publisher, unless otherwise indicated. Spectrum® is an imprint of Carson Dellosa Education. © 2015 Carson Dellosa Education.

Send all inquiries to:
Carson Dellosa Education
P.O. Box 35665
Greensboro, NC 27425

Printed in the USA
04-053217784

ISBN 978-1-4838-1197-0

Table of Contents Grade 2

Chapter 1 Writing a Story

Chapter 2 Writing to Inform

Table of Contents, continued

Chapter 3 Writing an Opinion

Chapter 1

Lesson 1 What Is Happening?

What is happening in these pictures? Write some words that tell what you see.

_____   _____

_____   _____

_____   _____

_____   _____

Lesson 1 What Is Happening?

Look at this picture. Then, read the sentence about the picture.

<u>Today is bath day for Buddy.</u>

The first word of a sentence begins with a capital letter. A sentence ends with a period. A sentence is also a group of words that tells a complete thought.

Now, look at the pictures below and on the next page. Write your own sentence about what is happening in each picture.

_____

_____

_____

_____

Lesson 1 What Is Happening?

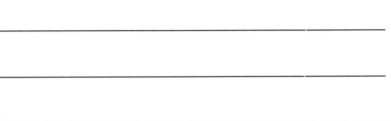

Ask a friend or adult to read your sentences. Does each sentence begin with a capital letter and end with a period? Go back and correct your sentences.

Lesson 2 I Feel. . .

How do you feel today? Do you feel happy, sad, or excited? Draw a picture that shows how you feel.

Now, write a sentence about how you feel. Add details about why you feel this way.

_____

_____

_____

_____

Lesson 2 I Feel. . .

Imagine it is your birthday. You have a big outdoor party planned. Now, however, it is raining. How do you feel? Draw a picture. Then, write a sentence telling how you feel.

_____

_____

_____

_____

Pretend that you just won a 200-mile bike race. You are very tired, but very excited. Someone just handed you a huge trophy. How would you feel? Draw a picture. Then, write a sentence about it.

_____

_____

_____

_____

Lesson 3 Your Five Senses

We use our senses to learn about the things around us. Sometimes, we use one sense. At other times, we use many senses. These are your five senses: **seeing**, **hearing**, **smelling**, **touching**, and **tasting**. How do you use them? Look at each picture. Circle the senses you could use to learn about the object in the picture.

seeing   hearing   smelling
       touching   tasting

seeing   hearing   smelling
       touching   tasting

seeing   hearing   smelling
       touching   tasting

Lesson 3 Your Five Senses

Imagine that you are one of the people in this picture. Use your senses to learn about everything around you. Write what you see, hear, smell, touch, and taste.

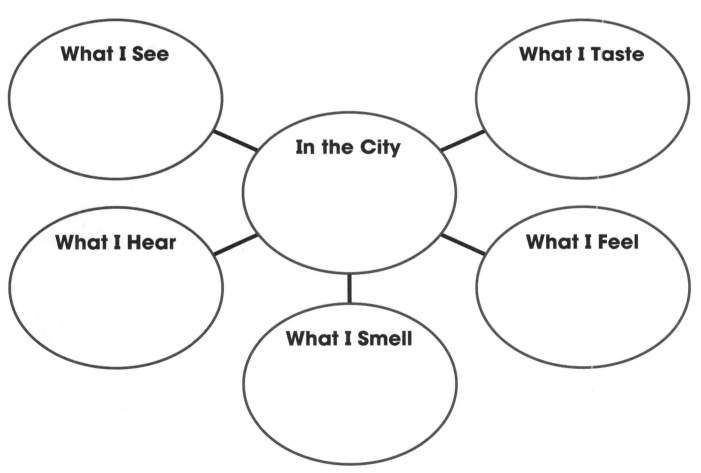

What I See

What I Taste

In the City

What I Hear

What I Feel

What I Smell

Lesson 3 Your Five Senses

Look at each picture. Name one sense you could use to learn about the object in the picture. Then, write a describing word that tells what you would learn from that sense. The first one is done for you.

<u>touch</u>   <u>rough</u>

_____   _____

_____   _____

_____   _____

Lesson 4 Use Describing Words

A **detail** is a small piece of information that helps readers "see" what you are writing about. To show details, writers use describing words that tell how something looks, sounds, smells, feels, or tastes.

Brian went to the zoo last week. Here's what he wrote.

The giraffe had a neck.

Notice that there are no words describing the giraffe's neck.

Brian added a describing word to help the reader "see" what he was writing about.

The giraffe had a neck.

Brian also wrote this sentence.

We ate popcorn and peanuts.

Brian then added a detail to describe the peanuts.

We ate popcorn and peanuts.

There was butter on Brian's popcorn. Rewrite Brian's sentence and add another word so the reader knows what the popcorn tasted like. Use this symbol (∧) to add your describing word.

_____

_____

_____

Lesson 4 Use Describing Words

Here is another sentence Brian wrote. What detail might make it better?

I didn't like the snake's skin.

How do you think the snake's skin felt? Add a describing word to Brian's sentence to tell how it felt.

Think about a place you have visited. Maybe it was a zoo or a fair. Or, maybe you watched a parade or went to a sporting event. Write describing words about it here.

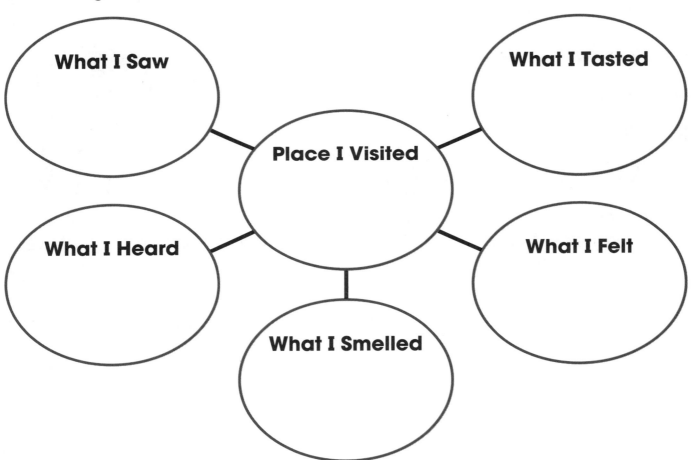

Did a friend or adult go with you? Ask someone who went with you to think of another describing word to add to your web.

Lesson 4 Use Describing Words

Now, write some sentences about the place you visited. Answer each question. Include at least one describing word in each sentence.

What did you see? Was it very colorful, pretty, or ugly?

_____

_____

What did you hear? Were there many kinds of sounds, or just a few?

_____

_____

What did you touch? Was it hard, bumpy, or sticky?

_____

_____

What did you smell? Were there many smells, or just one?

_____

_____

Did you have something to eat? How did it taste?

_____

_____

Have a friend or adult read your sentences. Does each sentence begin with a capital letter and end with an end mark?

Lesson 5 Describe It

Pretend that this pizza is sitting on the
table in front of you. You have just taken
your first bite. Write words that tell what
you see, hear, smell, feel, and taste.

I see _____

_____

_____

I hear _____

_____

I smell_____

_____

I feel _____

_____

I taste_____

_____

Lesson 5 Describe It

You can use many good describing words in a sentence. Here is a sentence that Kay wrote about the frog that she touched at the nature center.

The frog's slimy skin was cool, and his body was soft.

Think about that pizza again. Look at the words you wrote on page 16. Write a sentence about the pizza. Try to use at least two describing words in your sentence.

_____

_____

Now, think about another food that you like to eat. How does it look, sound, smell, feel, and taste? Write the name of the food. Then, write a sentence about that food. Use at least two describing words so your reader can really "see" the food.

Food _____

_____

_____

Ask an adult to help you use the Internet to find a photo of an interesting animal. Write a sentence about it using at least two describing words.

Animal_____

_____

_____

Lesson 6 I See a Place. . .

You see many places every day. What is one place you have seen today? Draw a picture of it. Then, write a sentence about the place. Use details to help your readers "see" the place.

_____

_____

Look back at your sentence. Does it begin with a capital letter? Does it end with a period? Is it a complete thought?

Lesson 6 I See a Place. . .

Dean wrote a sentence about his bedroom.

The walls are blue and have many things on them.

Dean did not help you see his room very well, did he? The blue part is good, but what do "many things" look like? We cannot tell because we do not know what "things" are.

Dean writes a new sentence.

The walls are blue and have many posters on them.

Now can you see Dean's room? We do not know what is on the posters, but at least we know what is hanging on the walls.

Think about your room. Write a sentence to describe it. Use words that describe just what you want your readers to see.

_____

_____

Questions to Ask About Descriptive Writing
Do your sentences include details?
Did you tell how something looked, sounded, smelled, felt, or tasted?
Does each sentence begin with a capital letter and end with an end mark?
Does each sentence have a complete thought?

Lesson 6 I See a Place. . .

Make up a place. It might be the perfect bedroom. It might be a forest on a distant planet. Draw a picture of your made-up place. Then, write one or two sentences about your place.

_____

_____

_____

Lesson 7 I Can Imagine

What if you could create a new planet? Would your planet have mountains? Would there be fields of corn? Would it have forests or oceans? Where would people live? Close your eyes and imagine a place on your new planet. Write some words that tell what you "see" in this place.

_____   _____

_____   _____

_____   _____

_____   _____

Imagine your planet again. What colors do you see? What do you hear and smell? What do things feel like? Write some words that tell how your planet looks, sounds, smells, and feels.

_____   _____

_____   _____

_____   _____

_____   _____

Lesson 7 I Can Imagine

Look back at the words you wrote on page 21. Tell about your planet. Write one or two sentences to answer each question. Remember to use your senses as you describe your planet.

What is the most beautiful part of your planet?

_____

_____

_____

Are there plants? If I touched one, what would it feel like?

_____

_____

_____

What does the sky look like on your planet?

_____

_____

_____

Type a description of your planet on the computer. Include a name for your planet. Choose a color and font that match your planet. Print your writing and share it with others.

Lesson 8 When Did It Happen?

Look at the pictures. You can tell what happens first, next, and last. Label the pictures in order. Write **first**, **next**, and **last**. These are called **time-order words**.

_____   _____   _____

_____   _____   _____

Lesson 8 When Did It Happen?

Now, write sentences to show the order of things.

Write one sentence about each picture. The first sentences are started for you.

First   Next   Last

First,_____

Next,_____

Last, _____

First   Next   Last

_____

_____

_____

Lesson 8 When Did It Happen?

In a story, writers usually tell what happens in order. First, one thing happens. Then, another thing happens, and so on. Practice telling about things that happen in order. Use words such as **next**, **before**, **after**, and **suddenly**.

What is happening in these pictures?

First,_____

Then, _____

Notice how the words **first** and **then** help keep things in order. Now, write two sentences about what is happening in these pictures. Use time-order words to tell the order in which things happen.

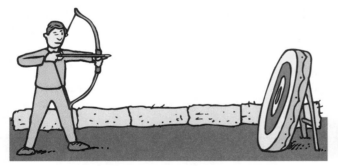 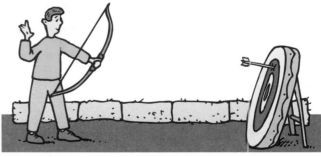

_____

_____

Lesson 8 When Did It Happen?

Now that you have everything in order, think about making your sentences interesting. Use details that help your readers "see" what is happening. Let's look at these two pictures again. Imagine you are writing a story about what is happening.

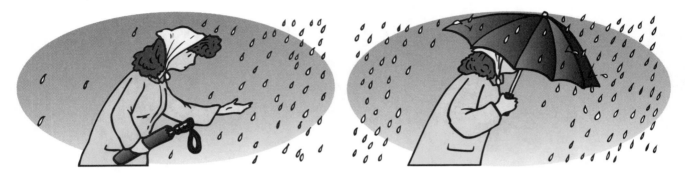

Write two more sentences about these pictures. Use words that tell how something looks, sounds, smells, feels, or tastes.

_____

_____

_____

Think about where this woman is. How might this place sound or feel or smell? Write a sentence about it.

_____

_____

Finally, write a sentence about the woman in the picture. How does she look or what could she be thinking?

_____

Lesson 9 Name That Story

The title of a story tells what the story is about. Read each story. Then, answer the question.

Holly is quiet all day. She won't talk or sing. She eats her food. She cleans her feathers. She seems to be waiting for something. What could it be? When Anna and Kenny get home, then we know. Holly says, "Where have you been? Where have you been?" Anna and Kenny laugh. Holly has been waiting for them all day.

1. What is the best title for this story? Circle your choice.

Anna and Kenny at School   Caring for a Parrot   Holly's Day

J.T. grinned all the way to school. He looked funny, but that was okay. Today was Mix-Up Day. His shoes didn't match. His wild pants did not match his striped shirt. Just to make sure, his shirt was on backward. When J.T. got to school, he saw a poster. It said, "Don't forget—Tomorrow is Mix-Up Day." J.T. stopped grinning.

2. What is the best title for this story? Circle your choice.

Mix-Up Day   J.T.'s Shirt   Signs at School

Lesson 9 Name That Story

Read the stories on this page. Then, read the titles in the box. Choose the best title for each story. Write the title on the line above the story. Remember to leave a space between each word.

Happy Landing	A Ride in Space	Rocket Launch
Space Race	Moon Monster	No One at Home

_____

The spaceship sailed through the sky. As Dale got close to the moon, he saw a strange sight. Another spaceship sat in his landing spot. Dale looked at his computer screen. The message said, "I win." Dale shook his head. His sister had beaten him to the moon again.

_____

Jan was looking forward to a good meal at the space station. It was almost time to land. She looked at her screen, then she looked again. There was nothing there. Jan tried to stay calm as she pushed buttons on the radio. There was no answer. The space station was gone.

Lesson 9 Name That Story

Here are two more stories. After you read each one, write a title on the line. Remember to leave a space between each word.

_____

Tina just had to tell about her prize. She called Kay. Kay said, "I can't talk right now. Can you come over in a little while?" Tina hung up. She still couldn't wait to tell. She walked to Kay's house. In the front yard were all of her friends. They were cheering for Tina. Everyone already knew about her prize.

_____

The batter smacked the ball, and Jim watched it fly up into the sky. He held out his glove and closed his eyes. Thump! Jim couldn't believe it. There was the ball, right in his glove. He raised his hand so everyone could see. Then, Jim couldn't believe it. He dropped the ball.

Lesson 10 Write About Today

Every day, something happens. On some
days, you do the same old things. On other
days, you do different things. It's fun to write
about what we do.

What have you done today? List what you have done.

_____   _____

_____   _____

_____   _____

Now, write some sentences about what you have done today.
Remember to use describing words so your readers can see, hear,
smell, feel, or taste what you did. Remember to put the events in order
using time-order words.

_____

_____

_____

_____

_____

_____

_____

Lesson 10 Write About Today

Now, list some things you know you will do later today.

_____   _____

_____   _____

Write about what you will do later today. Make sure to use time-order words. Begin each sentence with a capital letter. End each sentence with a period.

_____

_____

_____

_____

_____

Now, have a friend or adult read your sentences. Correct any that contain mistakes.

Questions to Ask About Descriptive Writing

Do your sentences include details?

Did you tell how something looked, sounded, smelled, felt, or tasted?

Does each sentence begin with a capital letter and end with an end mark?

Does each sentence have a complete thought?

Lesson 10 Write About Today

What is your favorite part of the day? Is it morning? After school? Draw a picture of something you do during your favorite part of the day.

What would you like to say about your favorite part of the day? Write about what is happening in your picture. When you are finished, ask yourself the questions on the bottom of page 31.

_____

_____

_____

_____

_____

_____

Lesson 11   What Is a Story?

Now that you are in second grade, you have already read lots of stories. You might even have written some stories. What is a story?

A story tells about people or animals. They are the **characters** in the story.

A good story is **fun** for the reader to read.

A story has a **beginning**, a **middle**, and an **end**.

A good story has **describing words** that tell about the characters, where the story takes place, and what happens.

Read this story. Think about what happens at the beginning, in the middle, and at the end.

A Day with Dad

Today is Saturday. Sue's mom has a meeting. So, Sue and Dad will spend the day together. Sue wonders what they will do.

First, Dad washes the dishes. Sue watches because she cannot reach. Then, Dad cleans the blue rug. Sue watches because the machine is too big. After that, Dad washes dirty windows. Sue watches because the windows are too high.

By lunchtime, Dad is worn out from working. Sue is worn out from watching. What can Sue do? Then, she has a great idea. Sue invites Dad to her room for lunch. Dad can just fit on Sue's little chair. And Sue can reach everything. It is the best lunch ever.

Go back and read the story again. Can you find the ending of the story? Circle it.

Lesson 11 What Is a Story?

Answer these questions about "A Day with Dad." Look back at the story on page 33 if you need to.

Who are the characters in the story?

_____   _____

What happens at the beginning, in the middle, and at the end of the story?

Beginning

Middle

End

How does the writer describe the rug and windows? Find these and other describing words. List them here.

_____   _____

_____   _____

_____   _____

Lesson 12 Write a Story

Look at the picture. Think of a story you might write about the people or the place in the picture.

These people are the characters in your story. Think of names for several of them.

_____   _____

_____   _____

Where are these people? Write some words that tell where they are. Also, write some describing words that tell about the sights, sounds, and smells of the place.

_____   _____

_____   _____

_____   _____

_____   _____

Lesson 12 Write a Story

Look at the picture on page 35 again. In the boxes, write ideas about what will happen in the beginning, in the middle, and at the end of your story.

Beginning

Middle

End

Lesson 12 Write a Story

Write your story here. Look back at the ideas you wrote on pages 35 and 36. Remember to give your story a title. When you finish, read your story and ask yourself the questions at the bottom of the page. If you can find ways to make your story better, write it again on another sheet of paper.

_____

_____

_____

_____

_____

_____

_____

Questions to Ask About a Story

Does the story have a beginning, a middle, and an end?

Did you use time-order words to make the order of events clear?

Did you use words that tell how things look, sound, smell, feel, and taste?

Is the story fun for your readers?

Does each sentence have a complete thought?

Does the story have a good ending?

Lesson 13 I Saw It All!

It is fun to tell about things that we have seen. Maybe you saw an interesting bird. Or, maybe you saw an amazing play at a football or baseball game.

Chase saw something amazing happen yesterday. Today at school, he wrote about it. First, he wrote down a few things to keep his ideas in order.

game with Mom
rain then wind
tree bending
back and forth
crack

Then, Chase wrote about what he saw. Here is his first draft.

It started to rain, and Mom called me into the house. We sat by the big window and played a game. Pretty soon, it started to get windy. We planted some new trees in the backyard last week. We watched the tree in the front yard. It bent back and forth. The wind blew the branches around. All of a sudden, there was a huge crack. Mom and I saw the tree fall. Now, our big tree is lying across the yard. Mom says the tree was old and rotten inside.

Look back at Chase's notes. Did he use those ideas in his writing? Find and circle them in Chase's first draft.

Lesson 13 I Saw It All!

Chase read his draft again. He decided he could make it better. He added words to help his readers see how the tree looked, both before it fell and as it fell. He also found a sentence that didn't belong. And he added a new beginning and a new ending.

> I was playing outside yesterday after school.
> It started to rain, and Mom called me into the house. We sat by the big window and played a game. Pretty soon, it started to get windy. ~~We planted some new trees in the backyard last week.~~ We watched the ^big oak tree in the front yard. It bent back and forth. The wind ~~blew~~ ^whipped the branches around. All of a sudden, there was a huge crack. Mom and I saw the tree ^slowly twist and fall. Now, our big tree is lying across the yard. Mom says the tree was old and rotten inside. ^I will miss that tree.

Think about something you have seen. Maybe it was something funny, something unusual, or something surprising. Write a few ideas here about what you saw. You might include some words that tell how something looked, sounded, smelled, felt, or tasted.

_____   _____

_____   _____

_____   _____

_____   _____

Lesson 13 I Saw It All!

Now, write about what you saw. Look back at what you wrote on page 39 to keep your ideas in order. Remember to include describing words so readers know how things looked, sounded, or smelled.

_____

_____

_____

_____

_____

_____

_____

_____

_____

Read your writing. Can you make it more interesting? Are there any ideas or sentences that don't belong? Make changes to your writing, like Chase did on page 39. Then, read your writing out loud to see how it sounds. Share your writing with someone who will enjoy it.

Lesson 14 The Writing Process: Story

"The Three Little Pigs" and "Snow White" are fairy tales. You probably know those and many other fairy tales as well. Sometimes it is fun to start with a story that everyone knows, and then make a new story about what happened next. For example, what happened to the Three Little Pigs? Did they all stay in the brick house? Where did the wolf go? And what about Snow White? What happened while she and the prince were living happily ever after? Did they ever visit the dwarfs? Or did the dwarfs go and live with Snow White?

Which fairy tales do you like best? Write their names here.

_____   _____

_____   _____

Think about how the fairy tales end. Ask yourself what happens next. Do you get any good ideas? Choose one fairy tale that you want to continue. Write its name and the names of the characters here.

Fairy tale _____

Characters _____

How does the fairy tale end? _____

_____

Write some ideas here about how you will add to the fairy tale.

_____

_____

Lesson 14 The Writing Process: Story

You are writing a story, so you need to have a beginning, a middle, and an end. Keep these things in mind:

- In the beginning of a story, readers meet the characters and find out there is a problem.

- In the middle, the action of the story takes place. The characters decide how to solve the problem.

- At the end, the problem is solved.

What will happen in your new fairy tale?

Beginning

Middle

End

Write the first draft of your fairy tale on page 43. When you are finished, ask yourself the questions at the bottom of the page. Then, make your story better. Make changes on page 43. Then, write a new copy on a clean sheet of paper or type it on a computer. Share your story with a younger child.

Lesson 14 The Writing Process: Story

_____

_____

_____

_____

_____

_____

_____

_____

_____

Questions to Ask About a Story

Does the story have a beginning, a middle, and an end?

Did you use time-order words to make the order of events clear?

Did you use describing words that tell how things look, sound, smell, feel, and taste?

Is the story fun for your readers?

Does each sentence begin with a capital letter and end with an end mark?

Does each sentence have a complete thought?

Chapter 1 Post-Test

Look at this picture.

Write two sentences that describe the place in the picture.

_____

_____

_____

Look at the pictures. Write **first**, **next**, and **last** to show what order the pictures should be in. Then, write about the pictures. Use time-order words to help your readers understand.

_____   _____   _____

_____

_____

_____

Chapter 2

Lesson 1 It Happened Because. . .

Why was Tess late for school? Why didn't Johnny turn in his homework? Why does the wind blow? When we write, we often tell why things happen.

Look at some pictures. The first picture shows what happened. The second picture shows why it happened.

This happened. . .   because. . .

Now, write **This happened** or **because** under the correct picture.

_____   _____

Lesson 1 It Happened Because. . .

Now, write about why things happen. Look at the pictures. Then, complete the sentence.

This happened. . .   because. . .

_____ because

_____ .

Did something happen to you today? Why did it happen? Draw what happened. Then, draw a picture that shows why it happened. Finally, write a sentence about what happened and why.

This happened. . .   because. . .

_____

Lesson 2 Explain It

When we write, we often tell, or explain, what happened. We usually tell what happened, and we tell why it happened. First, practice telling why. Answer these questions. Remember to put a period at the end of each sentence.

Why were you late?

I was late because _____

_____

_____

_____

Why are your shoes dirty?

_____

_____

_____

Why do you like that book?

_____

_____

_____

_____

Lesson 2 Explain It

Imagine that your picture is in the newspaper. Why would you like your picture to be in the newspaper? Did you invent something? Are you a hero? First, complete the sentence to tell why your picture is in the paper.

My picture is in the paper because _____

_____ .

Now, explain everything that happened. Give lots of details.

_____

_____

_____

_____

_____

_____

_____

_____

Lesson 3 Compare Them

When we think about how two things are the same and different, we compare them. Look at these pictures. Then, complete the sentences.

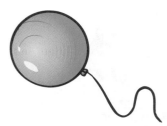   

These balloons are the same _____.

These balloons are different _____.

These cars are the same _____.

These cars are different _____.

These horses are the same _____.

These horses are different _____.

Lesson 3 Compare Them

Compare these boats. How are they the same? How are they different?

The first boat _____.

The second boat _____.

What is the same about these boys? What is different? Complete the sentences.

The first boy _____.

The second boy _____.

Now, compare your own hair color with the hair color of a friend or classmate. Complete these sentences.

My hair is _____.

The other person's hair is _____.

Are your hair colors the same or different?

Our hair colors are _____.

Lesson 3 Compare Them

These fish are the same size. What else about them can you compare? List some things here.

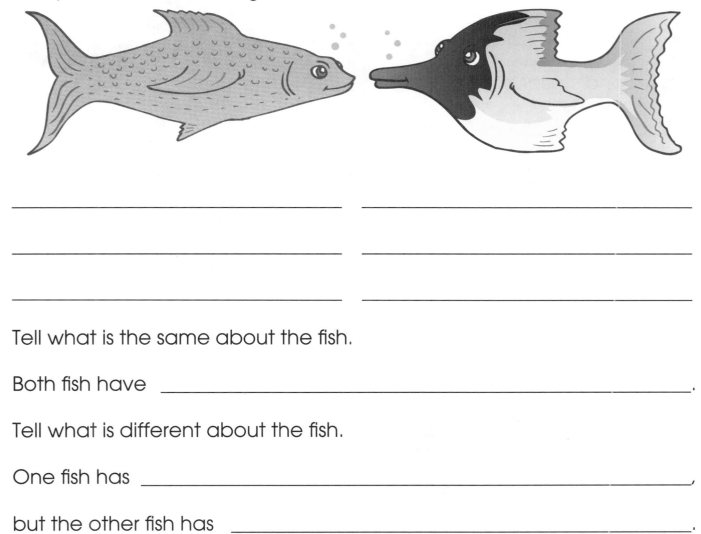

_____   _____

_____   _____

_____   _____

Tell what is the same about the fish.

Both fish have _____.

Tell what is different about the fish.

One fish has _____,

but the other fish has _____.

On Your Own

It is fun to compare things. Compare a playground ball with an orange. Compare a banana with a telephone. Choose two things and compare them. Make a list of how they are the same and how they are different on a separate piece of paper.

Lesson 4 Use Comparing Words

Compare these spiders. Tell which spider
is bigger and which is smaller.

The first spider is _____.

The second spider is _____.

Look at these pictures. Read the sentences.

The first ladder is **taller than** the second ladder.

The second ladder is **shorter than** the first ladder.

Now, use the words **taller than** and **shorter than** to compare these
pictures. Complete the sentences.

Dad is _____ Timmy.

Timmy is _____ Dad.

Lesson 4 Use Comparing Words

Look at the pictures. Write sentences that compare the objects in the pictures.

_____

_____

_____

_____

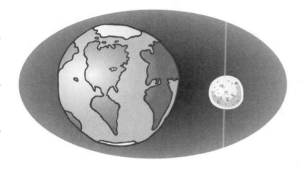

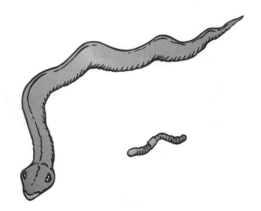

_____

_____

_____

_____

_____

_____

_____

Lesson 5 Alike and Different

Cayla is in second grade. In some ways, second grade is the same as first grade. In other ways, it is different. Cayla drew a chart and wrote down her ideas.

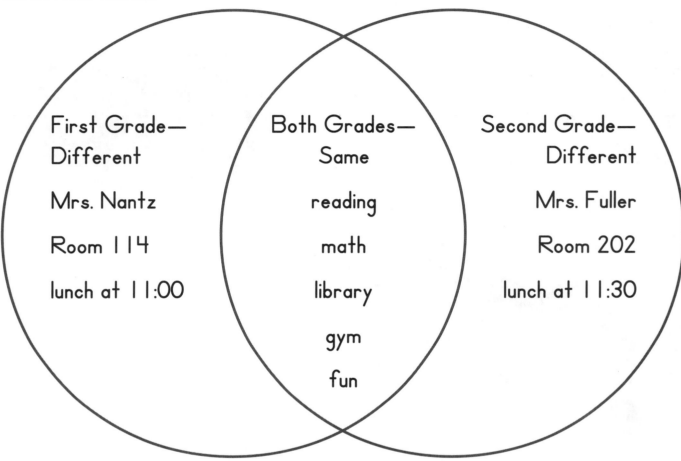

First Grade—
Different

Mrs. Nantz

Room 114

lunch at 11:00

Both Grades—
Same

reading

math

library

gym

fun

Second Grade—
Different

Mrs. Fuller

Room 202

lunch at 11:30

After she made her chart, Cayla wrote some sentences about first and second grade.

In first grade, I had Mrs. Nantz in Room 114.

Now, I have Mrs. Fuller in Room 202.

This year, lunch is later than last year.

Most of the classes are the same.

First grade was fun and so is second grade.

Lesson 5 Alike and Different

Think back to last year. What did you do in first grade? What did you learn? Write down everything you can remember.

_____   _____

_____   _____

_____   _____

Now, think about what is happening in second grade. How is second grade different from first grade? How are the grades the same?

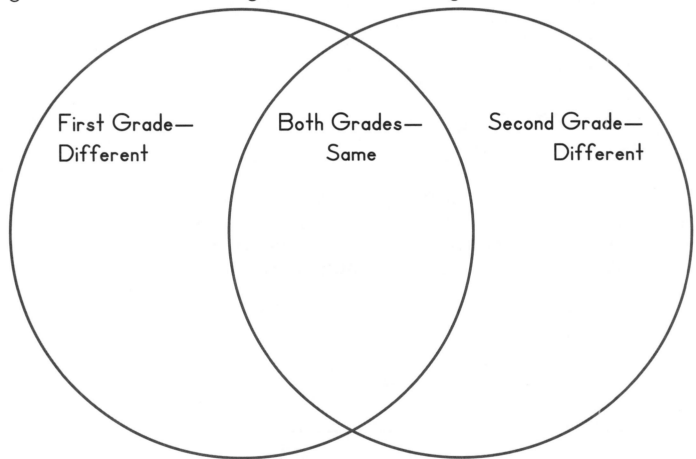

First Grade—
Different

Both Grades—
Same

Second Grade—
Different

Ask a friend who is your age to think about first and second grade. Does he or she have another idea to add?

Lesson 5 Alike and Different

Now, write some sentences that compare first grade and second grade. Use the ideas you wrote in the chart on page 55.

_____

_____

_____

_____

_____

_____

Look at your sentences again. Does each one begin with a capital letter? Does each one end with a period? Did you use good words to describe how something looked, sounded, or felt? Did you use any comparing words, such as **better than** or **later than**?

Ask a friend or adult to read your sentences and ask you a question. Answer the question here.

_____

_____

_____

_____

Lesson 6 The Writing Process: Friendly Letter

When you write a letter to a friend or grandparent, you are writing a friendly letter or e-mail. It is fun to write friendly letters. It's even more fun to get them. Maybe if you send a friendly letter or e-mail, you will get one back.

Tina wrote a friendly letter to her cousin Alice. As you read, think about why Tina wrote this letter.

July 17

Dear Alice,
    I just read your letter, and I am so excited. Mom and Dad are excited, too. You haven't been here for more than a year.
    I can't wait until you see my room. I got a bunk bed because Emily got her own room. You can have the top bunk!
    There are only 16 more days until you get here.
                    Love,
                    Tina

Tina wrote this letter because _____

_____ .

I might write a friendly letter because _____

_____ .

Lesson 6 The Writing Process: Friendly Letter

Look at Tina's letter again.

There is always a comma after the person's name.

There is a **date** at the top.

This is the **greeting**. The word **Dear** always begins with a capital letter.

This is the **body** of the letter.

July 17

Dear Alice,

    I just read your letter, and I am so excited. Mom and Dad are excited, too. You haven't been here for more than a year.

    I can't wait until you see my room. I got a bunk bed because Emily got her own room. You can have the top bunk!

    There are only 16 more days until you get here.

Love,

Tina

This is the **closing**. The word may be different, but there is always a comma after the word.

The person writing the letter always signs his or her name.

Questions to Ask About a Friendly Letter or E-mail

Is there a date?
Does the greeting begin with Dear?
Is there a comma after the person's name in the greeting?
Is there a comma after the closing?
Did you sign your name?

Lesson 6 The Writing Process: Friendly Letter

Think of someone you know. Write a letter to that person. Start with the greeting. Next, write the body of the letter. Then, write the closing. Look back at Tina's letter on pages 57 and 58 if you need to. In your letter, tell about something that happened and explain why. This will be your first draft. Later, you will have a chance to make your letter better and write a final copy.

_____

_____

_____

_____

_____

_____

_____

_____

_____

_____

_____

Lesson 6 The Writing Process: Friendly Letter

Now, look back at your letter on page 59. Is there anything you want to change? Could you add words that tell how something feels or looks?

Write your letter again. Make it even better. When you finish writing, ask yourself the questions on the bottom of page 58. Type your letter and send it as an e-mail.

_____

_____

_____

_____

_____

_____

_____

_____

_____

_____

_____

Lesson 7 The Writing Process: Thank-You Note

People write friendly letters for many reasons. One reason might be to thank someone for a gift. Here is a thank-you note that Brett wrote to his aunt.

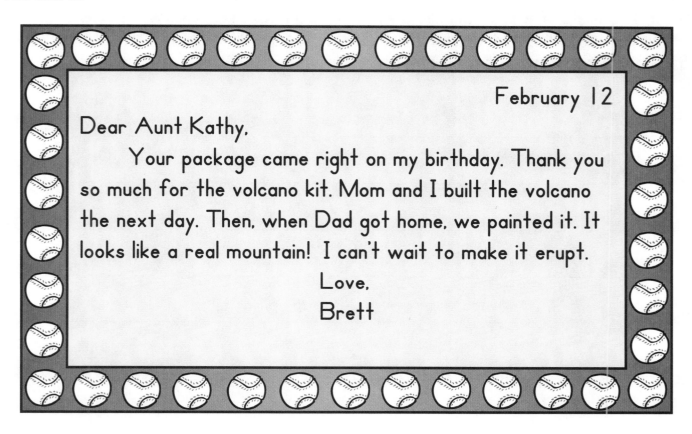

February 12

Dear Aunt Kathy,
    Your package came right on my birthday. Thank you so much for the volcano kit. Mom and I built the volcano the next day. Then, when Dad got home, we painted it. It looks like a real mountain! I can't wait to make it erupt.
                    Love,
                    Brett

Brett thanked his aunt nicely. He used the four parts of a friendly letter: date, greeting, body, and closing. He also told his aunt how he used her gift. Then, Brett wrote something special about the gift. He helped her "see" the gift by saying that "it looks like a real mountain!"

Think of some gifts you have received, or would like to receive. List them here.

_____   _____

_____   _____

Lesson 7 The Writing Process: Thank-You Note

Now, write a thank-you note for one of the gifts you listed on page 61. Start with the date and the greeting. Then, write the body. Remember to thank the person and to say something special about the gift. Use words to help the person "see" what you mean. Then, write the closing. This will be your first draft. Later, you will have a chance to make your letter better and write a final copy.

_____

_____

_____

_____

_____

_____

_____

Questions to Ask About a Thank-You Note

Is there a date?
Does the greeting begin with Dear?
Is there a comma after the person's name in the greeting?
Do you thank the person and name the gift?
Is there a comma after the closing?
Did you sign your name?

Lesson 7 The Writing Process: Thank-You Note

Now, look back at the draft of your thank-you note. Ask yourself the questions at the bottom of page 62. How can you make the note better? Could you add words that tell how something feels or looks?

Write your thank-you note again. Make it even better. Write your note in the space below or on a card. Send it in the mail to say "Thank you" to someone special.

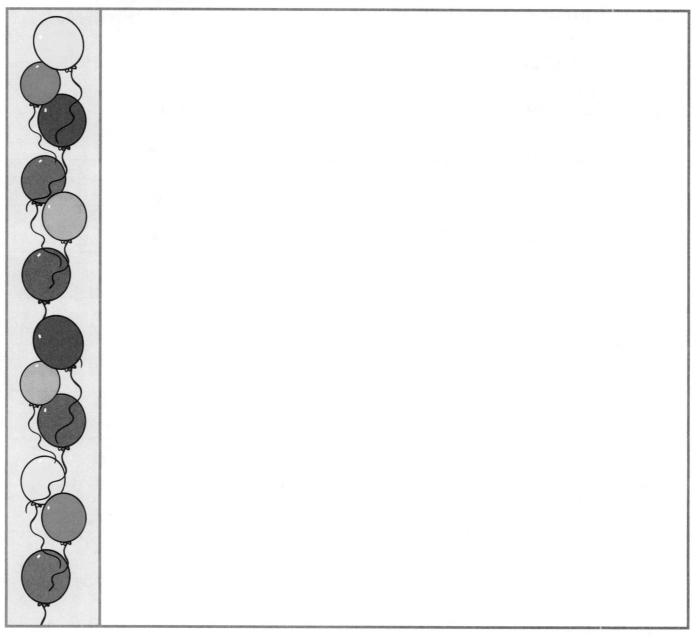

Lesson 8 You Can't Miss It

How do you get to a new place? You might follow a map or ask for directions. What if someone asks you for directions? Would you know how to give clear directions? Start by writing some words that you might use to give directions. Here are some words to help you get started. If you get stuck, think about how you get from one place to another.

first

next

then

last

finally

right

left

above

below

next to

Lesson 8 You Can't Miss It

Jim's mom is going to help the librarian at school tomorrow. She has asked Jim for directions to the library. Here is what Jim wrote.

> First, sign in at the table by the front door. Then, go straight ahead to the office. Turn right and go to the end of the hallway. Turn left and go to the third door on the left. Enter the library.

Jim gave his mom good directions. He used time-order words and many direction words. Circle the words that tell when. Underline the words that tell where.

Can you give directions to the library in your school? Close your eyes and imagine going from your school's front door to the library. Write the directions here.

_____

_____

_____

_____

_____

Ask a friend to read your directions. Did you use time-order words? Did you use direction words? Did you forget anything?

Lesson 8 You Can't Miss It

Now, give directions to another place in your school. Help someone find your classroom, the lunchroom, the gym, or another area of the school that you like. Remember to use time-order words as well as direction words. Look back at your list on page 64 if you want to.

_____

_____

_____

_____

_____

_____

_____

_____

_____

_____

Look back at what you wrote. Make sure that each sentence begins with a capital letter and ends with a period.

Lesson 9 This Is How

Sandy likes to make paper flowers. She wrote down the steps she uses to make them.

Sandy used clear words so readers know exactly what to do.

Sandy numbered the steps so the order is clear.

Sandy included all of the steps.

Sandy included an ending.

Paper Flowers

1. First, cut tissue paper in squares.
2. Put the end of a pencil in the center of a paper square.
3. Wrap the paper around the pencil.
4. Remove the pencil.
5. Finally, put a green pipe cleaner on the bottom of the flower for a stem.

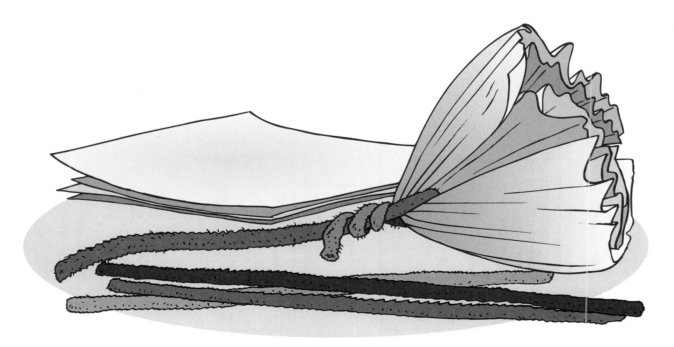

Lesson 9 This Is How

What do you know how to make or do? Maybe you know how to make something out of clay. Maybe you know how to plant flowers. Think of the steps it takes. Draw the steps in order. If you need more space, use another sheet of paper.

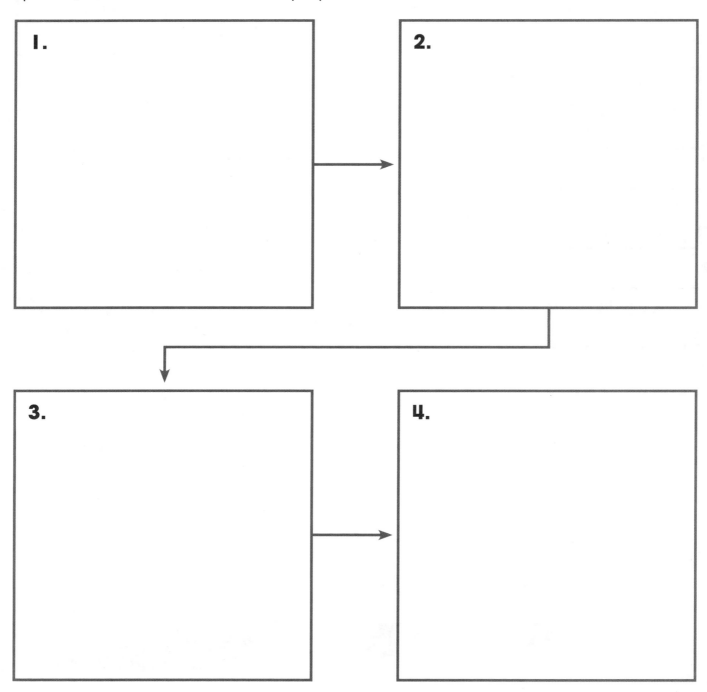

Lesson 9 This Is How

Look back at the pictures you drew on page 68. Now, write the steps. Remember to number your steps. Use clear words so that your readers know exactly what to do. Make sure to include an ending.

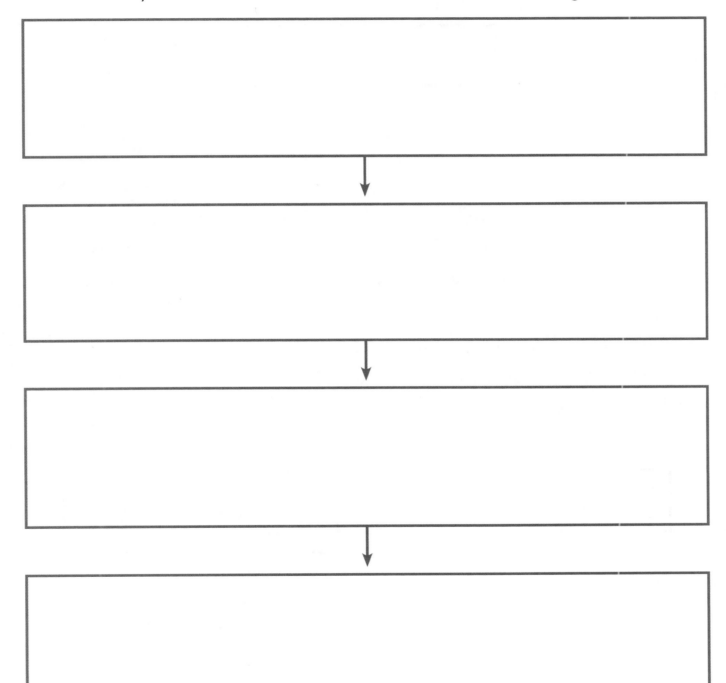

Lesson 10 You Are an Expert

Sandy already listed the steps for making paper flowers. Now, she wants to write a complete set of instructions. Here is what she wrote.

Sandy added describing words to be more clear.

Sandy L.

March 14

How to Make a Tissue Paper Flower

First, cut a square piece of ^colored tissue paper. For a small flower, use a 2-by-2-inch square. For a large flower, use a 5-by-5-inch square. Then, place the end of a pencil in the center of a square. Next, wrap the paper ^eraser around the pencil. Remove the pencil. Finally, ~~put~~ ^twist a green pipe cleaner ^gently onto the bottom of the flower for a stem.

Sandy changed **put** to **twist** because it tells what to do with the pipe cleaner.

Sandy added a word that tells how something should be done.

Lesson 10 You Are an Expert

Think again about what you know how to do. Use your idea from pages 68 and 69, or choose a different idea. Make sure you know all the steps. Write your steps here.

_____

_____

_____

_____

_____

_____

_____

Questions to Ask About How-to Writing

Did you put the steps in order?

Did you include all of the steps?

Did you use order words to make the order clear?

Did you use clear words that tell what things look like or how to do things?

Does each sentence begin with a capital letter?

Does each sentence end with an end mark?

Did you include an ending?

Lesson 10 You Are an Expert

Ask an adult to read what you wrote on page 71. Ask: Is there anything I need to change? Are the steps in order? Could I add words to make something more clear? Does every sentence help you understand?

Write your directions again. Make them even better. When you finish writing, ask yourself the questions on the bottom of page 71.

_____

_____

_____

_____

_____

_____

_____

_____

_____

_____

_____

Lesson 11 Find Out About It

One way to find out about something is to ask a question. Take a close look at this question.

What kind of cloud is that?

Circle the first letter of the question. It is a capital letter.

Circle the mark at the end of the question. It is a question mark.

Notice that the question is a complete thought.

Here is another question. Circle the capital letter at the beginning. Circle the question mark at the end.

Do you think it will rain?

Now, read this question. Something is missing.
Add the question mark at the end.

When will the rain end

Greg corrected the next question. He knew that the first letter should be a capital letter. So, he drew three little lines under the letter and wrote the capital letter above it. He also added a question mark at the end.

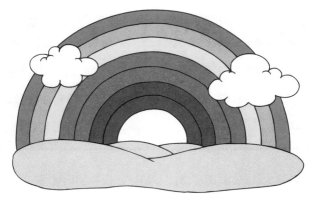

Lesson 11 Find Out About It

What would you like to find out about the weather? Write your own question here.

_____

_____

Now, look at these pictures. Ask some questions. Some questions are started for you.

What color is _____

How big is _____

_____

_____

Questions to Ask About a Question

Does it begin with a capital letter?
Does it end with a question mark?
Does it tell a complete thought?

Now, look back at your questions. Correct any sentences that contain mistakes.

Lesson 12 The Writing Process: Report

Martha made a list of the things she knows about the sky.

sky is blue	stars at night
sun during day	clouds day or night
moon at night	

There are some things Martha wants to find out about, though. She listed them here.

wind	puffy clouds
gray clouds	stringy clouds
white clouds	

What do you know about? Maybe you know about a certain animal or maybe you know how to play many different kinds of games. Make a list of things you know about.

_____   _____

_____   _____

_____   _____

_____   _____

_____   _____

_____   _____

Lesson 12 The Writing Process: Report

Look back at the list you wrote on page 75. Choose one idea. Now, list what you know about it.

What I Know About: _____

_____   _____

_____   _____

_____   _____

_____   _____

_____   _____

What else would you like to find out about the topic? Write questions.

_____

_____

_____

_____

_____

_____

Lesson 12 The Writing Process: Report

Ask a librarian to help you find three books that could answer the questions you wrote on page 76. Write the titles of the books.

1. _____

2. _____

3. _____

What other way could you learn about your topic? Circle one.

Have an experience by doing something or going somewhere.

Ask a knowledgeable adult.

Ask an adult to help you look for a good Web site.

Now, read the books and learn about your topic in other ways. You might find the answers to your questions. Or, you might find answers to questions that you didn't think of before! This is called doing **research**. On the lines below, write three interesting facts you learned about your topic.

1. _____

_____

2. _____

_____

3. _____

_____

Lesson 12 The Writing Process: Report

Remember the topic you wrote about on the last two pages. What did you already know about it? What did you learn from your research?

Plan a report about your topic. Write a few words on each line below to plan your report.

Title: _____

My report is about: _____

_____

_____

Interesting fact #1: _____

_____

Interesting fact #2: _____

_____

Interesting fact #3: _____

_____

Why this topic is important: _____

_____

_____

Lesson 12 The Writing Process: Report

Follow the plan you made on page 78 to write your report on the lines below. Begin by explaining what your report is about. Then, write interesting facts about your topic. Include details and descriptive words, too. Give your report a good ending by telling why your topic is important.

_____

_____

_____

_____

_____

_____

_____

_____

Questions to Ask About a Report

Does it have a good beginning?
Does it include facts?
Does it include details and descriptive words?
Does it have a good ending?
Does it have complete sentences?

Lesson 12 The Writing Process: Report

Read what you wrote on page 79. Ask yourself the questions at the bottom of the page. Ask a friend or adult to read your report and answer the questions, too. What can you change to make your report even better?

Write a final copy of your report on the lines below. Or, type your final report on a computer. Make an illustration or find a photograph to illustrate your report. Then, share it with a reader.

_____

_____

_____

_____

_____

_____

_____

_____

_____

_____

Chapter 2 Post-Test

Write a friendly letter to someone you know. Explain ideas about something or tell how to do something. Include a beginning, middle, and end. Your letter should have all the parts shown on page 58.

_____

_____

_____

_____

_____

_____

_____

_____

_____

_____

_____

Chapter 3

Lesson 1 Facts and Opinions

An **opinion** tells how a person feels about something. It might tell that you like or dislike something. It might state that something is interesting or boring. It can tell that something is pretty or ugly. Complete the sentences below to write opinions.

The best thing to do after school is _____.

The nicest flowers are _____.

I think snakes are _____.

Each person has his or her own feelings and opinions. Sometimes, you want others to agree with your opinions. You may want a friend to play the game that you want to play. Or, you may want your family to choose your favorite meal for dinner. Others may be more willing to agree with your opinion if you explain why you feel the way you do.

Read Trina's opinion below.

Cats are not fun to be around because they make me sneeze.

Why doesn't Trina like cats? _____

Complete the sentences to explain your opinions.

The best thing to do after school is _____

because _____.

I think snakes are _____

because _____.

Lesson I Facts and Opinions

Opinions and facts are different. An opinion tells the way you feel about something. A fact tells something that is true and can be proven.

Fact: Earth is a planet.

Opinion: Earth is the most interesting planet.

Read the sentences. If the sentence states a fact, write **F** beside it. If the sentence states an opinion, write **O** beside it.

_____ An animal doctor is called a veterinarian.

_____ Riding a bike is more fun than riding a scooter.

_____ *Diary of a Worm* is a great book.

_____ Winning is the most important part about playing a game.

_____ An ostrich egg is bigger than a baseball.

_____ January has 31 days.

_____ Mint chocolate chip is the best ice cream flavor.

_____ Reptiles are gross.

Many opinions contain feeling words such as **best**, **bad**, **ugly**, **fun**, or **delicious**. Circle a feeling word in each opinion above.

Lesson 2 The Best Holiday

Every year there are many holidays. What holidays do you celebrate? Write them on the lines below. If you need more ideas, look at a calendar.

_____   _____

_____   _____

_____   _____

_____   _____

Now, look at your list of holidays. Which one do you think is the best? Circle your favorite.

Draw yourself celebrating the holiday.

Lesson 2 The Best Holiday

Look at the holiday you circled on page 84. Why is it your favorite? Complete the sentence.

This holiday is the best because _____

_____

_____

_____

_____ .

Think of another reason it is the best and write it below.

_____

_____

_____

Think of one more reason it is the best and write it below.

_____

_____

_____

_____

Lesson 2 The Best Holiday

You have opinions about the best holiday and reasons for your opinions. Writers can join opinions, reasons, and other ideas using **linking words** like the ones below.

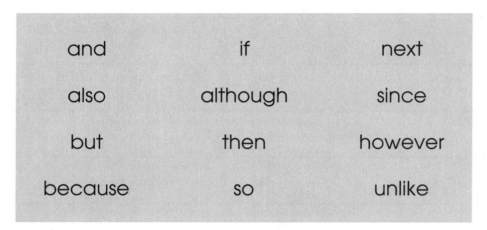

and	if	next
also	although	since
but	then	however
because	so	unlike

Read the sentences Eli wrote about his favorite holiday. Circle the linking words.

Thanksgiving is the best holiday. It is my favorite because we eat turkey and mashed potatoes. I also like Thanksgiving because my grandma, grandpa, aunt, and uncle come over for dinner. I am never bored on Thanksgiving since I can play with my cousins.

Lesson 2 The Best Holiday

Now, write about why you think the holiday you chose is the best. State your opinion. Give good reasons for your opinion. Use linking words to join your ideas. Include a good ending that will make your readers agree with you.

_____

_____

_____

_____

_____

_____

_____

_____

_____

_____

_____

Lesson 3 Which Game?

Imagine that you will spend time with two friends. What game or activity will you do together? Complete the sentence to state your opinion.

I think we should play _____.

Draw a picture of you and your friends playing the game you chose.

Lesson 3 Which Game?

Think about the game you chose on page 88. Why would you like to play it with your friends? Write five reasons below. Draw a star in the box beside three reasons you think your friends will agree with most.

☐ _____

_____

☐ _____

_____

☐ _____

_____

☐ _____

_____

☐ _____

_____

Lesson 3 Which Game?

On the lines below, write a letter to your friends. Convince them to play the game you want to play. State your opinion. Give three good reasons you feel the way you do. Use linking words to connect ideas. Write a good ending that will make your friends agree with you.

_____

_____

_____

_____

_____

_____

_____

Read your letter.

• Does it give good reasons for your opinion?

• Do your sentences begin with a capital letter?

• Do your sentences end with an end mark?

Type your letter on a computer and send it as an e-mail to your friends.

NAME _____

Lesson 4 Write a Book Review

Think of books you have read. Write their titles on the lines below.

Funny Books   **Sad or Scary Books**

_____   _____

_____   _____

Exciting Books   **Interesting Books**

_____   _____

_____   _____

Look at the books you named. Which one do you think someone your age would like the best? Draw a star beside its title.

Think of good reasons why someone your age should read this book. Finish the sentences below. Write the least important reason first. Save the most important reason for last.

You will like _____

because _____.

You will also like _____

because _____.

The most important reason you will like _____

is because _____.

Lesson 4 Write a Book Review

Write a book review on the lines below. Try to convince a person your age to read the book you chose. State your opinion. Use linking words to join your opinion with reasons. Save your most important reason for last. End with a strong statement about the book.

_____

_____

_____

_____

_____

_____

_____

Questions to Ask About Opinion Writing

Did you state your opinion?

Did you give good reasons for your opinion?

Did you use linking words?

Did you write a strong ending?

Does each sentence have a complete thought?

Does each sentence begin with a capital letter and end with an end mark?

Lesson 4 Write a Book Review

Ask a friend or adult to read the book review you wrote and answer the questions at the bottom of page 92. Did your review make your reader want to read the book? Can you add anything to make your writing stronger?

Write your book review again. Make it even better.

_____

_____

_____

_____

_____

_____

_____

Share Your Writing

You should be proud of your book review! Choose a way to share it with others.

• Ask a librarian if you can display your review at the library.

• Ask a bookstore manager if you can display your review on a bulletin board at the store. Do not include your name.

• With an adult's permission, type your review as a comment at an online bookstore. Do not include your name.

Lesson 5 The Writing Process: Opinion Letter

What job would you like to do when you grow up? Would you like to be an inventor? A ship's captain? A chef? In the box, draw yourself doing your future job.

Complete the sentences to write three reasons you would like to have this job.

1. I want to be a _____ because

_____.

2. I want to be a _____ because

_____.

3. I want to be a _____ because

_____.

Lesson 5 The Writing Process: Opinion Letter

You will write a letter to your future self about the job you should have. Your letter will give opinions and reasons for your opinions. It may also include facts about the job you want to have someday.

Circle one way you will find facts about your job.

   Talk to someone I know who has this job.

   Read a library book about the job.

   Ask an adult to help me find a good Web site about the job.

Carry out your research to find facts about the job you want to have. Write three facts below.

I. _____

_____

_____

2. _____

_____

_____

3. _____

_____

_____

Lesson 5 The Writing Process: Opinion Letter

Read Rahm's letter below. He wants to be a police officer someday. Underline the sentences that state opinions. Draw a star beside the facts. Circle the linking words.

Dear Rahm,

    I hope you are reading this when you are almost an adult! Don't forget that you should become a police officer. One reason is that you like to exercise. Officers must work out and stay fit. Unlike boring jobs, being a police officer is exciting. Officers patrol different places and talk to different people every day. Finally, being a police officer is the best job for you because it is a way to help people. Officers keep people safe. Since you are almost grown up, it is time to start training for your perfect job. You will be a great police officer!

                  Your friend,

                  Rahm (age 9)

Do you think Rahm's future self will agree with his opinions? Why or why not?

_____

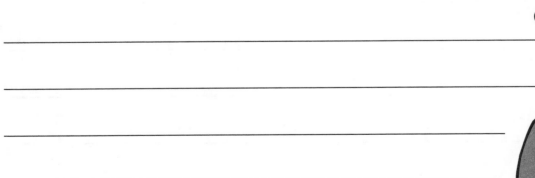

Lesson 5 The Writing Process: Opinion Letter

On the lines below, write a letter to your future self. Use the letter on page 96 as a model. Use the opinions and reasons you wrote on page 94. Use the facts you wrote on page 95. Try to make your future self agree with your opinions. Make sure your letter has a strong ending.

_____

    _____

_____

_____

_____

_____

_____

_____

               _____

               _____

Read your letter and ask yourself the questions on page 92. Is there anything you need to change to make your writing better? Write a final copy of your letter on a sheet of paper. Seal it up in an envelope. Put it in a safe place where your future self will find it!

Chapter 3 Post-Test

Read the sentences below. If the sentence is a fact, write the letter **F** next to it. If the sentence is an opinion, write the letter **O** next to it.

_____ The cactus is the most interesting desert plant.

_____ The cactus is the most common desert plant.

_____ There are over 2,000 different kinds of cacti.

_____ Lemons grow on trees.

_____ Lemonade is the best summer drink.

What do you think is the best summer treat to eat or drink? Why? Write your opinion below. Give good reasons.

_____

_____

_____

_____

_____

_____

_____

Writer's Handbook

When should I use a capital letter?

The first word of a sentence always begins with a capital letter.
> **T**he kitten jumped into my lap.

The word **I** is always spelled with a capital letter.
> Kristen and **I** laughed at the kitten.

The name of a person or an animal always begins with a capital letter.
> The kitten belongs to **K**risten.
> The kitten's name is **M**eep.

Other kinds of names also begin with capital letters. Here are some examples:
> streets: **M**artin **A**venue   **J**effers **R**oad
> schools: **J**ackson **E**lementary **S**chool
> towns and cities: **M**edford   **R**ome
> states: **W**isconsin   **G**eorgia
> countries: **C**anada   **I**taly
> holidays: **L**abor **D**ay
> days and months: **T**uesday   **J**uly
> clubs and groups: **C**ub **S**couts   **V**alley **G**arden **C**lub
> companies: **D**oggie **D**ay **C**are   **F**oster **P**aint **C**ompany

What are the rules about sentences?

A sentence must always tell a complete thought.
> Complete thought: She meowed.
> Complete thought: The kitten yawned and rolled over.
> Not a complete thought: She again.
> Not a complete thought: Around and around her.

Writer's Handbook

A sentence always begins with a capital letter.
> **C**arry the kitten carefully.

A sentence always ends with an end mark. There are three kinds of end marks. A sentence that tells something ends with a period.
> The kitten is soft**.**

A sentence that asks something ends with a question mark.
> Is the kitten soft**?**

A sentence that shows excitement or fear ends with an exclamation point.
> The kitten scratched me**!**

What is the writing process?

Writers use five steps when they write. These steps make up the writing process.

Step 1: Prewrite

First, writers think up ideas. This is called **prewriting**. They might write their ideas in a list. They might even make a chart and put their ideas in order.

Sam will write about his trip to the zoo. He put his ideas in a web.

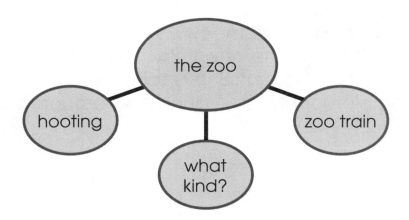

Writer's Handbook

Step 2: Draft

Next, writers put their ideas on paper. This is called a **first draft**. Writers know that there might be mistakes. That's okay. Most writers do not get everything perfect on the first try.

Here is Sam's first draft.

> ## Zoo Noises
>
> Every time I go, I learn something new. I went to the zoo three times last year. last week, I learned that there are many noises at the zoo. There was a funny hooting sound. I asked what kind that was Then, my brother told me it was the train whistle. I felt pretty silly. I wonder what I will learn next time I go to the zoo.

Step 3: Revise

Then, writers change or fix their first draft. This is called **revising**. They might move ideas around or add information. They might take out words or sentences that don't belong. Here are the changes that Sam made.

> ## Zoo Noises
>
> ~~to the zoo~~
> Every time I go, I learn something new. ~~I went to the zoo three times last year.~~ last week, I learned that there are many noises at the zoo. There was a funny hooting sound. I asked what kind that was
> of animal
> Then, my brother told me it was the train whistle. I felt pretty silly. I wonder what I will learn next time I go to the zoo.

Writer's Handbook

Step 4: Proofread

Writers usually write a new copy so their writing is neat. Then, they look again to make sure everything is correct. They look for mistakes in their sentences. This is called **proofreading**.

Sam wrote a new copy. Then, he found two last mistakes.

Zoo Noises

Every time I go to the zoo, I learn something new. last week, I learned that there are many strange noises at the zoo. I heard a funny hooting sound. I asked what kind of animal that was. Then, my brother told me it was the train whistle. I felt pretty silly. I wonder what I will learn next time I go to the zoo.

Step 5: Publish

Finally, writers make a final copy that has no mistakes. They are now ready to share their writing with a reader. They might choose to read their writing out loud. They can add pictures and create a book. There are many ways for writers to **publish**, or share, their work with readers.

Here is the final copy of Sam's writing about the zoo.

Zoo Noises

Every time I go to the zoo, I learn something new. Last week, I learned that there are many strange noises at the zoo. I heard a funny hooting sound. I asked what kind of animal that was. Then, my brother told me it was the train whistle. I felt pretty silly. I wonder what I will learn next time I go to the zoo.

Writer's Handbook

What different kinds of writing are there?

Writers sometimes write about things they have done or seen. They might tell about something funny, sad, or unusual. When Sam wrote about what he saw at the zoo, he was writing about real things that he did and saw.

Look at Sam's zoo story again.

The word **I** shows that the writer was part of the action.	A time-order word shows the order of events.

Zoo Noises

Every time I go to the zoo, I learn something new. Last week, I learned that there are many strange noises at the zoo. I heard a funny hooting sound. I asked what kind of animal that was. Then, my brother told me it was the train whistle. I felt pretty silly. I wonder what I will learn next time I go to the zoo.

Describing words help readers "see" or "hear" what is happening.

The writer stayed on topic. All of the sentences give more information about a zoo noise.

Writers sometimes write about made-up things. They might write about people or animals. The people and animals might seem real, but the writers made them up. Here is a made-up story that Shawn wrote.

Time-order words help keep ideas in order.

Describing words help readers "see" what is happening.

Shawn's Zoo

Shawn wants to be a zookeeper. Right now, he keeps small animals. He pretends that his mice and his cat are zoo animals.

Some day, he will keep big animals. He watches his gray mice running on their little wheel. At his zoo, Shawn will teach elephants to run on a big wheel. His cat chases a ball. At Shawn's zoo, the lions will play soccer against the tigers.

Shawn has lots of ideas for his zoo. He thinks his zoo will be a great zoo.

Shawn's readers will have fun reading his ideas.

The writer stayed on topic. All of the sentences give more information about a made-up zoo.

Writer's Handbook

Writers sometimes write about how to do things. They might tell how to play a game or make a snack. Sam has a favorite snack. He wrote about how to make it.

The steps are all in order, starting with the items needed to make the snack.

Order words help readers keep the steps in order.

Clear words help readers understand what to do.

Cracker-Cheese Surprise

First, set out wheat crackers, sliced olives, sliced cheese, and a metal pie plate. Lay out some crackers in the pie plate. Then, place one olive slice on each cracker. Place one slice of cheese on top of each cracker. Finally, ask a grown-up to set the pie plate under a broiler. Heat just until the cheese bubbles. Have the grown-up remove plate from broiler and let cool for several minutes. At last, you get to enjoy your healthy snack.

Writers sometimes write to describe things. They might tell about an object, a place, or an event. They use good sense, or describing, words so that readers can see, hear, smell, feel, or taste whatever is being described. Read how Sam described his snack.

Sizzle helps readers hear what is happening.

Warm helps readers know how the snack feels.

Bubbly helps readers see what is happening.

Salty helps readers taste the snack.

I can tell when my snack is done because I hear a little sizzle from the oven. When my mom opens the broiler door, the cheese is bubbly. I can hardly wait for the crackers to cool. When I take a bite, the cracker crunches and the warm cheese stretches out in a long string like taffy. And then, that salty little olive slice is just waiting to surprise me. Yum!

Writer's Handbook

Writers write friendly letters to share news or ideas. They also write letters to get information. A friendly letter has four parts: the date, the greeting, the body, and the closing. Here is a letter Sam wrote to a friend about something that happened at the zoo.

| Words in the greeting each begin with a capital letter. | There is always a comma after the person's name. | The date is in the upper, right corner. |

August 26

Dear Kyle,

    Last week, while you were at camp, we went to the zoo. We had a great time.

    The best part was the elephants. Did you know that elephants love to take baths? The elephant keeper was spraying a hose at the elephants. The water shot up in a big spout. The elephants stood under the water just as if they were taking a shower. Then, one of them started to dance. Before long, all three of them were dancing in the shower!

    It's only a week until school starts. I'll show you my dancing elephant pictures on the first day of school.

Your friend,
Sam

The body of the letter gives information.

Only the first word of the closing begins with a capital letter. There is always a comma after the closing.

The writer signs his or her name.

Answer Key

Chapter 1

Lesson 1

Page 5
Answers will vary.

Page 6
Sentences will vary.

Page 7
Sentences will vary.

Lesson 2

Page 8
Pictures will vary.
Sentences will vary.

Page 9
Pictures will vary.
Sentences will vary.

Lesson 3

Page 10
Circled senses: seeing, smelling, touching, tasting
Circled senses: seeing, hearing, smelling, touching
Circled senses: seeing, smelling, touching

Page 11
Responses will vary.

Page 12
Possible responses: smell—skunk odor
hearing—water OR smell—fish, etc.
feeling—cold

Lesson 4

Page 13
Responses will vary.

Page 14
Responses will vary.

Page 15
Responses will vary.

Lesson 5

Page 16
Responses will vary.

Page 17
Responses will vary.

Lesson 6

Page 18
Pictures will vary.
Sentences will vary.

Page 19
Sentences will vary.

Page 20
Pictures will vary.
Responses will vary.

Answer Key

Lesson 7

Page 21
Responses will vary.
Responses will vary.

Page 22
Responses will vary.

Lesson 8

Page 23
first, next, last
next, last, first

Page 24
Sentences will vary.

Page 25
Sentences will vary.

Page 26
Sentences will vary.

Lesson 9

Page 27
Circled titles:
Holly's Day
Mix-Up Day

Page 28
Space Race
No One at Home

Page 29
Responses will vary.

Lesson 10

Page 30
Responses will vary.
Sentences will vary.

Page 31
Responses will vary.
Sentences will vary.

Page 32
Pictures will vary.
Sentences will vary.

Lesson 11

Page 33
Circled ending: It is the best
lunch ever.

Page 34
Sue, Dad
Beginning: Sue wonders what she
and Dad will do.
Middle: Dad works while Sue
watches.
End: Sue invites Dad to eat lunch
in her room.
Describing words: blue, big, dirty,
high, little, best

Lesson 12

Page 35
Responses will vary.

Answer Key

Page 36
Responses will vary.

Page 37
Stories will vary.

Lesson 13

Page 38
Circled words or phrases: rain, played a game, get windy, bent back and forth, crack

Page 39
Responses will vary.

Page 40
Responses will vary.

Lesson 14

Page 41
Responses will vary.

Page 42
Responses will vary.

Page 43
Stories will vary.

Post-Test

Page 44
Sentences will vary.
next, first, last

Chapter 2

Lesson 1

Page 45
because, This happened

Page 46
Sentences will vary.
Pictures will vary.

Lesson 2

Page 47
Answers will vary.

Page 48
Explanations will vary.

Lesson 3

Page 49
These balloons are the same size.
These balloons are different colors.
These cars are the same color.
These cars are different sizes.
These horses are the same size.
These horses are different colors.

Page 50
Answers will vary.

Page 51
Answers will vary.

Lesson 4

Page 52
The first spider is bigger than the second.
The second spider is smaller than

Answer Key

the first.
Dad is taller than Timmy.
Timmy is shorter than Dad.

Page 53
Responses will vary.

Lesson 5

Page 55
Responses will vary.

Page 56
Sentences will vary.

Lesson 6

Page 57
Tina wrote this letter because her cousin is coming to visit.
Sentences will vary.

Page 59
Responses will vary.

Page 60
Responses will vary.

Lesson 7

Page 61
Responses will vary.

Page 62
Responses will vary.

Page 63
Notes will vary.

Lesson 8

Page 64
Lists will vary.

Page 65
Circled words: First, Then
Underlined words: by, front, ahead, right, end, left, left
Responses will vary.

Page 66
Responses will vary.

Lesson 9

Page 68
Pictures will vary.

Page 69
Steps will vary.

Lesson 10

Page 71
Steps will vary.

Page 72
Directions will vary.

Lesson 11

Page 73
What kind of cloud is that?
Do you think it will rain?
When will the rain end?

Answer Key

Page 74
Responses will vary.

Lesson 12

Page 75
Responses will vary.

Page 76
Responses will vary.
Questions will vary.

Page 77
Titles will vary.
Circled ideas will vary.
Facts will vary.

Page 78
Responses will vary.

Page 79
Reports will vary.

Page 80
Reports will vary.

Post-Test

Page 81
Letters will vary.

Chapter 3

Lesson 1

Page 82
Responses will vary.
Trina does not like cats because

they make her sneeze.
Responses will vary.

Page 83
F, O, O, O, F, F, O, O
Circled words: fun, great, most
important, best, gross

Lesson 2

Page 84
Responses will vary.
Drawings will vary.

Page 85
Responses will vary.

Page 86
Circled words: because, and,
also, because, and, since

Page 87
Responses will vary.

Lesson 3

Page 88
Sentences will vary.
Drawings will vary.

Page 89
Responses will vary.

Page 90
Letters will vary.

Answer Key

Lesson 4

Page 91
Titles will vary.
Sentences will vary.

Page 92
Reviews will vary.

Page 93
Reviews will vary.

Lesson 5

Page 94
Drawings will vary.
Sentences will vary.

Page 95
Responses will vary.
Facts will vary.

Page 96
Underlined:
Don't forget that you should become a police officer.
Unlike boring jobs, being a police officer is exciting.
Finally, being a police officer is the best job for you because it is a way to help people.

Starred:
Officers must work out and stay fit.
Officers patrol different places and talk to different people every day.

Officers keep people safe.

Circled:
when, Unlike, Finally, because, since

Page 97
Letters will vary.

Post-Test

Page 98
O, F, F, F, O
Responses will vary.